SPECIAL EDUCATION: WHAT & WHY?

DR DHEERAJ MEHROTRA
DR AMITA PANDIT BHATT

Made with ♥ on the Notion Press Platform
www.notionpress.com

Contents

Preface *v*

1. Special Education: A Priority 1
2. Case Studies On Special Education & Care 14
3. Tips To Parents Of Special Children 96

About The Authors 103

Preface

Special Education: What & Why? is a priority for schools, educators and parents. Special education creates possibilities for students, fostering achievement and accomplishment. Students with impairments have a substantial number of challenges, but they can attain their full academic potential provided they get adequate assistance in overcoming these challenges. Only when these people have access to the specialized instruction and support provided via special education will they be able to attain academic and social success?

When students with disabilities can accomplish their educational objectives with the assistance of special education teachers, it may improve their sense of self-worth and their sense of accomplishment. This, in turn, may positively impact the student's overall health. This book explores special education's what, why, and significance, including real-world examples and lessons learned from those experiences.

@Authors

ONE

SPECIAL EDUCATION: A PRIORITY

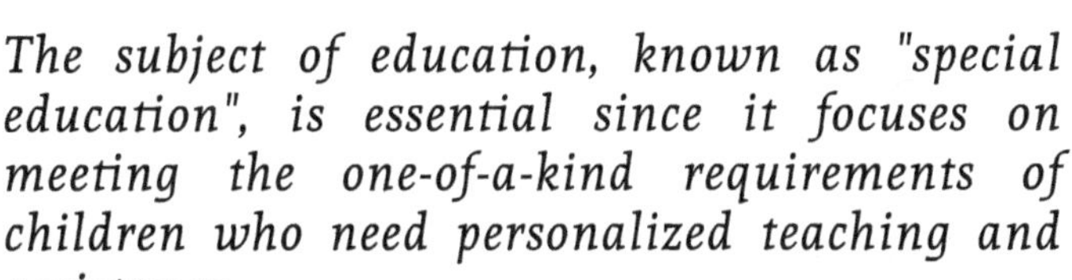

The subject of education, known as "special education", is essential since it focuses on meeting the one-of-a-kind requirements of children who need personalized teaching and assistance.

These children often suffer impairments, developmental delays, behavioural or emotional issues, or learning difficulties. For these children to realize their full potential, specialist assistance is required. Providing equitable educational opportunities to all children, regardless of the skills or disabilities of those students, is the primary goal of inclusive education, of which special education is an essential component.

The following arguments underline the importance of special education in schools.

First, Special Education ensures that all kids have equal educational opportunities. Every kid has the right to get an education tailored to their requirements and interests. Students who have disabilities are protected from falling further behind in their education or being denied access to the educational system using the provision of special education. It offers these kids customised assistance to study and succeed in their academic and social endeavours.

Second, kids with impairments may get specialized education and assistance via the Special Education program. Students do not all learn in the same manner, and for children with disabilities to attain their full potential, they often need specialized education and assistance. Helping children with disabilities achieve academic success is the goal of Special Education, which offers various support services, including individualized teaching, tutoring, and access to specific learning resources.

ART

Finally, individuals with disabilities are taught essential life skills via the Special Education program. Not only does Special Education place emphasis on academic accomplishment, but it also emphasizes the development of skills that are essential to being successful in life. Communication, socializing, problem-solving, self-advocacy, and self-determination are some examples of abilities that fall under this category. Students with impairments are better able to succeed in their personal and professional lives when they get training in these areas via the Special Education program.

Fourthly, inclusiveness and diversity are encouraged via special education. Inclusive education is based on the fundamental notion

that all students, regardless of their skills or impairments, should be allowed to study alongside one another and achieve academic success. By the provision of appropriate assistance to children with impairments, Special Education plays an essential part in the process of fostering inclusion. Special education helps break down barriers and promotes awareness and acceptance of diversity by integrating children with disabilities into the regular classroom environment.

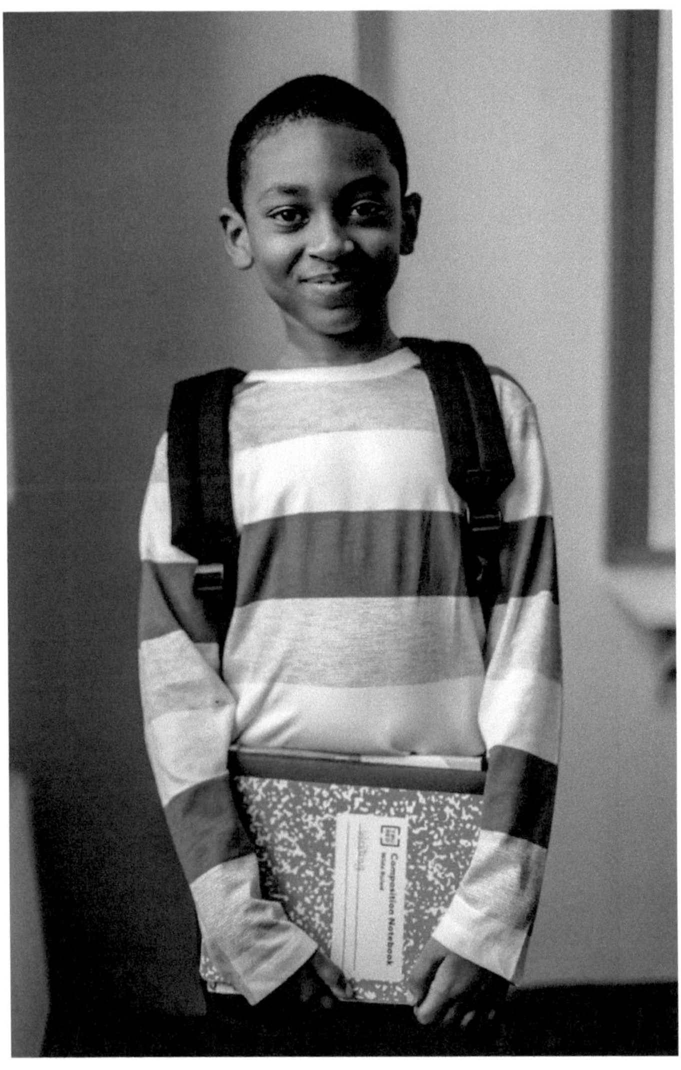
Composition Notebook

Fifthly, Special Education helps families in many different ways. Families with children with impairments often confront particular problems, including monetary, emotional, or social difficulties. Not only does Special Education provide help to kids who have impairments, but it also offers support to the families of those students. A common component of special education is providing training and support for parents, as well as counselling services and information about available resources to assist families in coping with the obstacles they confront.

Sixthly, Special Education encourages success and accomplishment by providing opportunities. Students who have impairments encounter a significant number of obstacles, but if they get enough help, they are capable of realizing their full academic potential. These individuals can only achieve academic and social success when they can access the specific teaching and assistance offered via special education. Special education may boost students' self-esteem and give them a feeling of achievement, which can benefit their general health by assisting students with disabilities in achieving their academic goals.

In conclusion, Special Education is an essential component of Inclusive Education, which ensures that all students, regardless of their talents or impairments, have equal access to educational opportunities. The goals of special education are to encourage specialized teaching and assistance, educate essential life skills, promote inclusion and diversity, provide support for families, and encourage success and accomplishment. Students with impairments would not have access to the appropriate help to study and succeed if it were not for Special Education. As a result of this, it is very crucial for schools to continue to place emphasis on special education and to make available the resources required to assist kids who have impairments.

TWO

CASE STUDIES ON SPECIAL EDUCATION & CARE

An- Introduction

Special education is a word used to describe educational programs and services offered to kids with disabilities, learning challenges, or other specific academic requirements. This might include pupils who are deaf, blind or have further hearing or speech impairments. Students with special needs may benefit from the assistance offered by these programs and services, which are intended to provide them with the support they need to achieve academic, social, and emotional success.

Students of any age may use action services, starting as early as preschool and continuing through high school. An Individualized Education Program (IEP) is how special education is delivered in the United States. This education is supervised by federal law (IEP). The Individualized Education Program, often known as an IEP, is a legal document that

specifies the particular educational requirements of a student and the services that will be given to satisfy those needs.

A kid can be classified as needing special education services if they have one of many distinct kinds of impairments or learning challenges. The following are some of the most frequent types of disabilities:

Learning disabilities hinder a student's ability to read, write, or do mathematical calculations. A student's capacity to digest information and effectively communicate may also be negatively impacted due to these factors.

Intellectual disabilities hinder students' ability to acquire new knowledge and process what they have already learned. Problem-solving, decision-making, and abstract thought may be challenging for students with intellectual limitations.

Emotional and behavioural disorders influence a student's social and emotional well-being. These disorders may be divided into two categories: Adolescents who struggle with emotional and behavioural problems may find it challenging to regulate their impulses, cope with anger, and communicate appropriately with others.

Autism spectrum disorders are a group of developmental conditions that hurt a pupil's social and communicative abilities. Children with autism spectrum disorders could have trouble communicating verbally and nonverbally, having social relationships, and engaging in repetitive activities.

In addition to these more prevalent forms of disability, there are various additional circumstances in which a student may be eligible for special education services. Impairments of hearing or vision, physical limitations, and attention deficit hyperactivity disorder are some examples of these conditions (ADHD).

Various environments are suitable for delivering special education services depending on the student's requirements. Some kids may get assistance in the same classroom as their peers enrolled in general education. In contrast, others may receive benefits in a separate classroom or a facility dedicated to special education. In some circumstances, pupils could get care in their homes or at local hospitals.

Special education services are developed to cater to the specific requirements of each student, regardless of the location where they are provided. This may include changes to the course material, acquiring specialised hardware or technology, and extra assistance from instructors and other trained experts.

The participation of parents and other caretakers is often regarded as one of the aspects of special education that is of the utmost significance. Parents significantly impact the individualised education program (IEP) created for their child and are essential members of the team that delivers special education services. Parents and teachers can ensure that kids with special needs get the assistance they need to thrive in school and beyond by collaborating to serve these students' needs better.

To summarise, special education is essential to the overall educational system. It was developed to cater to the specific requirements that children with disabilities and other types of special needs have. Special education aims to assist children in achieving academic, social, and emotional success by providing specialised education programs and various support services. It is vital to ensure that all children have access to the education they need to realise their full potential, which is why it is essential.

CASE STUDY ON *Developmental Delay #1*

Sunil Chellaram, now a ten-year-old boy, had delayed development since birth due to Cerebral Palsy. His family hails from Yarab Nagar, Bangalore, from a low-income stratum. The household needs are entirely dependent on the daily wage obtained by his father.

He was referred to MI in 2009, and though he was then four years old, he could hardly sit or stand independently. To address this concern, Standing Frame and Ankle Foot Orthosis were provided.

He could stand upright with wall support using the devices and regular therapy for two years. The next goal was to make him walk with permission, for which a Reverse Walker was suggested.

He has attended Public School for four years and is presently a first-grade pupil. His mother says, "Today, after nine years of struggle, he can walk independently. He has come a long way in achieving a few milestones and has miles to go before he achieves them all".

Encouragement, support and guidance motivate Shahin Parveen to dream like any other girl her age.

Five-year-old Shahin Parveen comes from a poor family. During one regular home visit, Shahin was identified with brittle bones that restricted her mobility. She could not walk and would drag herself to move around in the home. As such, her social life was limited to the four walls of her home. Like any other kid, she dreamed of making new friends and playing with them. Unable to do so, Shahin started slipping into depression.

Her left leg was deformed, and there was no possibility of correcting her deformity through any surgery. After a series of assessment sessions, the appropriate assistive device for her could be suggested. She was provided with bilateral Ortho-Prosthesis, auxiliary crutches and a walker. Apart from this, she also received therapy interventions and guidance. She gained confidence gradually, and her social life improved too.

The next phase was to encourage her to enrol in school. To make things easy, Makatab E. Primary school was made accessible. Finding new friends and interacting with them helped her widen her horizon. She was seen participating in extra-curricular activities.

Currently, Shahin can perform all her activities independently. She can climb two to three steps which were, at a point, only a dream. She studies in class six at Moulana Hasraat Mohani Memorial Girls High School. Support and encouragement helped Shahin improve her functional ability and continue her studies like any other girl her age.

Roopa's Inspiring Progress

Twelve-year-old Roopa studies in 5th standard at GLPS. Children have one or more favourite teachers in school, and so does Roopa. Looking back at Roopa's life, we can understand why she adores her teacher Suneethamma.

Roopa, the second born to her parents, could not speak till six years and was utterly dependent on her mother for daily activities. On assessment, she was identified with mental retardation and speech impairment.

Though Roopa was admitted to school, community members and teachers were initially apprehensive regarding her ability to study. During that time, MI intervened and oriented her parents to initiate Activities of Daily Living for Roopa.

With support from the Education Department of Chamrajnagar, an orientation programme for teachers on implementing inclusive education was conducted. The programme has formulated an individual education plan according to Roopa's abilities.

In the meantime, Suneethamma's capability to see beyond Roopa's impairment has helped her receive individual attention for her learning. Roopa has shown significant improvement in her studies and actively participates in extra-curricular activities.

Case Studies of Autism Spectrum Disorders #2

Lokesh is a 12-year-old boy who was diagnosed with ASD at age 2. Lokesh is generally healthy, although he has recently been diagnosed with rheumatoid arthritis and is sensitive to pain. He struggles with small spaces and "bottlenecks" where many people are assembled. Lokesh participates in special education at a local elementary school. His strengths include being curious, social, and visually astute. His challenges include communication, impulsivity, and behaviour that may include tantrums, aggression, and property destruction. These challenges have made it difficult for Lokesh to participate in activities with peers.

Communication Profile

Lokesh has a positive-behaviour support team and receives the speech-language intervention. He is a multimodal communicator whose verbal communication is not understood by most people. He uses a Palm, pictures, personal signs, gestures, and some words to communicate.

Assessment

Lokesh's communication was assessed. As a criterion-referenced, curriculum-based tool, it determines a child's profile of strengths and needs based on his or her developmental stage in social communication and emotional regulation. Lokesh was in the Language Partner stage of communication. We collected data in three contexts: school, home, and an intervention session in the clinic.

Social Communication

Lokesh's strengths in social communication included engaging in reciprocal interactions, sharing attention to regulate the behaviour of others, and using several modes of communication. His needs in social touch included sharing a range of emotions with symbols and sharing intentions for joint attention by commenting on objects, actions, and events or requesting information across partners and contexts.

Emotional Regulation

Lokesh's emotional regulation strengths included responding to assistance from a familiar partner he trusted, recovering from extreme dysregulation with support from a regular partner, and using a behaviour strategy (holding a block of wood) to remain focused and calm in some familiar environments. His needs in the area of emotional regulation were seeking assistance with emotional regulation from others, responding to service across contexts, and responding to the use of language strategies across environments.

Transactional Support

Transactional support was strong in some areas. For example, all of Lokesh's partners wanted him to learn and communicate more conventionally, and he had consistent, responsive communication partners at home. Lokesh needed the same responsive style across all partners and the constant use of visual and organizational supports to enhance learning and comprehension of language and behaviour.

Intervention

Goals included:

** Increased use of emotional words.*

** Commenting on objects, actions, or events.*

** Choosing what he needs to calm himself from the choices offered.*

Transactional goals included:

** Using augmented input.*

** Providing a binder with a schedule and social stories.*

** Making devices always available and using an interactive diary developed by his mother.*

These supports were implemented in activities of interest to Lokesh, such as holidays, his life in photo albums, tools, and events at home.

Outcomes

In the past two years, Lokesh has made many communication gains. His device has more than 200 pages of icons, which he accesses independently to express feelings. He has told us when he is angry, happy, sad, frustrated, and sick, and he engages in reciprocal exchanges, commenting on the shared object or event of interest. He has started to mark tense when he comments by using the "later" and "past" icons on his device to clarify his message. He can tell his partner what he needs to calm himself when choices are offered. In addition, he has more responsive communication partners who can provide him with the learning support he needs.

Case Study of Student Identified with an Intellectual Disability #3

Brief History

Kesha was served through an IEP since preschool. She also was connected to the Board of Developmental Disabilities (BDD) before age two and received Early Intervention services through the BDD. She attended the integrated preschool in her local school district and continued participating in school until graduation. Throughout her educational career, Kesha required IEP services and support. She accepted the assistance of others to navigate the school, make decisions, and prepare before for class or other activities. Kesha's social circle and activities have always been essential to her life.

Early Discussions;

During their early middle school years, Kesha strongly desired community employment. Kesha and her family had discussions as early as elementary school that focused on 'working' as part of her future adult life. However, even as she entered high school, she struggled to narrow her interests to begin a specific career plan.

In School Support

When Kesha attended the integrated preschool in her local school district, she received related speech, occupational and physical therapy services through the program. In their elementary years, she continued to be served through an IEP and received academic support, related services and organisational and social skills assistance. This assistance continued through middle and high school but expanded beyond academic subjects to vocational skills and activities.

As Kesha moved into high school, the related services were primarily consultative and focused on her adult goals and the skills and needed support for adult life.

In middle school, she began her transition planning with a multi-agency team. At this time, the team found she was receiving a great deal of assistance from both teachers and paraprofessionals to complete her academic assignments and prevocational tasks. This included support in organizing materials and facilitating social engagement with peers. She was able to care for all her personal needs during the school day.

The following information reviews the multi-agency information gathered to inform transition assessment and to develop the postsecondary goals.

Family Engagement

Recognizing that a general family outreach procedure is insufficient to meet many individual families' needs is essential. Throughout Kesha's journey, team members focused on engaging Kesha's family in meaningful future planning using various strategies and resources. This included offering ongoing and timely information while assisting the family in understanding and connecting to resources. The team was also sensitive to the family's priorities and goals and used these to help guide the planning. The family's needs changed over the years, requiring the school and agencies' continuing efforts and strategies to evolve.

Transition Assessment:

Information was collected by a multi-agency team using the following tools and methods:

Transition Assessment Tools and Processes Included:

- *Student interest inventories using easy-read materials, pictures and videos*

- *Student interview, multiple opportunities, shortened sessions.*

- *Job Shadows in employment environments identified from interest inventories*

· Review previous years' records to identify strengths, practical supports and areas of need. Community-based work assessment

· Observations in multiple environments – school, home, community – for independent living skills, social competencies, level of independence, problem-solving, and communication.

· Interview with parents/family members and teachers from previous years

· Review of information from the Individual Service Plan through the County Board of DD to inform Preferences, Interests, Needs, Skills/ Strengths (PINS)

Preferences/ Interests:

- Spending time with friends and family playing games,

- going to the mall and doing crafts

- Shopping for clothes, looking at clothes, fashion,

- watching TV shows about fashion

- Would instead work with others than alone.

- Prefers individual instruction in new tasks or learning new skills

- Interested in pet animals, such as cats, small dogs and birds

- Enjoys the creativity of fixing hair and makeup (with her mom and sister)

- Enjoys meeting new people Skills/Strengths

- Emerging interest in cooking - especially baking

- Can articulate what she prefers and does not

- prefer to teachers and sometimes parents

- Can follow a visual schedule to complete routine

- Understands information best using easy-read materials & picture symbols

- Hygiene and appearance are excellent

tasks of independent living

- Motivated to learn when instruction and experiences are designed for her learning style

- Able to use a calculator for basic math

- Learning to follow essential recipes (using picture supports) to bake cookies and other desserts.

Needs/Challenges;

- Vocational tasks attempted at school require ongoing

- adult prompting and extended time to complete correctly

- Academic subjects present a challenge.

- Kesha • requires specially-designed instruction and modification of all content areas

- Problem-solving in new situations is stressful. Lacks confidence in new situations

- Becomes anxious/stressed when trying new tasks. Concerned with making a mistake. Looks for assistance before trying.

- Requires assistance to remember and use safety measures in the kitchen (at home)

- Independent with personal care needs in school and home

- Social skills are a strength. Most confident with adults.

- Difficulty narrowing her interests to begin a specific career plan

- Requires extended time and support to transfer or apply skills and knowledge to new situations.

Case Study of specific learning disabilities #4

NAME: Harshita

Date of Birth: 29 / 4 / 2003

Father's name: Sh. Sohan Lal (Age 45 years). He is in a government job and has studied until class 10.

Mother's name: Mrs Sita Thakur (Age 38 years). She is a homemaker and has also studied until class 10.

Mother Tongue: Hindi

Another language: Pahari

Religion: Hindu

Locality: Urban

Type of family: Joint

Number of members in the family: 12

Sibling: Older brother aged 12

Cardinal position of child: Second

Problem noted first: At the age of 7 years

APRIL-MAY, 2014.

Pregnancy: Wanted

No infection to the mother during pregnancy.

Proper feeding in the neonatal period: Yes

Baby respiration: Normal

Adequate immunisation for mother: Yes

Any infection at birth: No

Head injury: No

Convulsions: No

Jaundice: No

From the above investigation, one realises there was no problem during pregnancy, and the pregnancy was a wanted one. The special teacher at Udaan reported that Harshita is a very social child. She enjoys the company of her peers. She likes to do her work first of all. She enjoys controlling her group. She conducts the morning assembly very well too. She is loud and clear in her voice. She likes to participate in every activity, like dancing, singing etc.

Earlier, she studied in a regular school in Ghanahati (a place on the outskirts of Shimla). But her teachers could not help her much due to her inability to learn. They would make her know, but she would be blank the next moment. It was frustrating for the teachers and parents since their efforts went down the drain. It was then suggested to the parents that the girl be shifted to a school which provided extra help to the child.

A school for special children where teachers are specially trained to take care of these children. At Udaan, her teachers spend a lot of time with her. They repeat the same thing time and again. They do not pressure her to learn and remember too many things simultaneously. They allow the child to learn at her own pace, so they do not get stressed. Also, she is given positive reinforcement at regular intervals to encourage her to learn. Whenever she can memorise, she is given a reward in the form of praise or a sweet. This dramatically boosts her morale, and she takes even more interest in her work.

Harshita joined Udaan in 2013. In one year, she has improved considerably in her writing and reading. She can write English and Hindi words. She is better at Hindi than English. She knows the names of animals, days of the week, months of the year, people at work etc. But she can write these things only when some hint is provided. She can write five lines about herself and her mother. She can also write a few lines on everyday stuff like cows. She copies from the blackboard accurately. About mathematics, she can do 3-digit addition sums. Also, 3-digit subtraction sums and multiplication sums with single digits have been taught to her. She knows the tables till 5. The teacher is going slow with her, so she can learn only a few things but memorise them well. Along with this, she is also taught the names of everyday items which one uses.

According to the teacher, Harshita is a compassionate child who feels hurt if scolded or ridiculed. So the only mantra with her is love and patience.

The parents, too, have a very positive attitude towards the child. She takes a keen interest in all the school activities and ensures that the child keeps abreast of all that is being done there. She provides full help and supports to her. This is evident from some charts that she helped her make. The father, too, takes an interest in all her activities. The parents want the child to become independent and make their daughter do some vocational course or training to earn her livelihood easily, even when they might not be around.

CONCLUSIONS;

The child does suffer from a special kind of learning disability which we label as executive functioning, wherein a child forgets as soon as he learns. This condition is very restricting as the child cannot equal other children even though the I.Q. level may not be poor. Such a child needs repetition of the content that is taught time and again.

He cannot retain what he has learnt for an extended period. In such a situation, the teacher and parents must be patient with him and devote time to the child so that he revises, again and again, to memorize well.

Again, scolding and reprimanding will not help, as the child will only get demoralised as he is already trying his best and cannot do better.

Also, comparing him with others would put him on the back foot.

Case Study of multiple Disabilities #5

Vinod is a 14-year-old 8th-grade student diagnosed with severe and multiple disabilities. He has cerebral palsy and epilepsy. He takes medicine to control his seizures and has had several surgeries to improve his ability to walk without falling. Vinod is also nonverbal because his cerebral palsy affected his ability to control his lip and tongue movements in speaking. He struggles with poor fine motor skills and has difficulty with other school activities, such as holding a pencil, writing, and using a calculator. Vinod also needs considerable modifications in the curriculum in the general education classroom. However, he can ride a bicycle, use the computer, listen to popular music, read his level books, and do chores around the house. Currently, an IEP team is trying to decide what will be best for Vinod throughout high school. He wants to live away from home and enjoys being with his friends.

Critical Characteristics of Individuals with Severe Disabilities

Abstract thinking/Conceptual Characteristics:

- Difficulty learning information that is abstract and figurative thinking

Learning Characteristics:

- Takes longer, and they need more opportunities to learn

- Will learn fewer skills and gain less knowledge

Attention Characteristics:

- Difficulty completing tasks for a certain amount of time

- Trouble focusing

Memory Characteristics:

- Lack of working memory and short-term memory

- Can remember people, events, knowledge, and skills

Transfer/Generalization Characteristics:

- Cannot take newly learned knowledge and skills and use them in a new environment or apply the learning in some manner that was not directly taught

- Need to be shown how to apply the skills

Communication Characteristics:

- Lack of communication skills

- Delayed speech or language

- Need communication systems to assist them

Social and Personal Characteristics:

- Important for students to be included to help form social bonds with peers

- Quality of life has been linked to social relationships

Behavioural Characteristics:

- Repetitive, non-purposeful movement (i.e. rocking, flapping hands)

- Self-injurious behaviour

- Mostly due to communication challenges

Physical Characteristics:

- Health impairments – heart and respiratory problems and orthopaedic disabilities

- Physical disabilities – can be progressive, leading to early death, and compromise a student's ability to interact with their environment and people

Students with Deaf/Blindness:

- Social adjustment and behaviour

- Sensory needs, learning, mobility, social interactions, academics

Academic:

When addressing Vinod's academics, I would need to know his academic abilities. I need to talk to his parents and be well-informed about his IEP. Since Vinod is in 8th grade, his IEP should already state all of his goals and what support Vinod will need in the classroom. It would also be beneficial if I talked to his previous teachers. The teachers could provide information on where Vinod is struggling the most. When I know Vinod's academic ability, I can modify the curriculum to meet his needs for his success.

Social and Emotional:

As Vinod's teacher, it is vital for me to understand his emotional well-being. Certain situations might upset him or cause him to stress out, and I need to be aware and prepared for any of the triggers he might have. I also need to ensure his classroom peers include him. Vinod has been with some of his classmates since kindergarten, and they enjoy helping him out. I need to know who they are for me to partner Vinod up with his friends for group projects.

Communication:

As his teacher, Vinod is nonverbal, and I must understand his communication. I will need to be able to communicate with Vinod about the lesson, specific directions and assignments. I will need to be aware of any technology he uses to communicate. For example, if he uses an IPad to talk, I will need to understand how to work it and respond appropriately to him. This information should also be provided on his IEP as part of his support and services.

Medical:

All teachers need to know a student's medical history. The parents should provide a list of any medication a student is taking to the nurse, and the teachers should have access to the information and knowledge of when they need to take it. As Vinod's teacher, it is crucial for me to be aware that he has epilepsy and that he is currently on medication to control it. Since he takes it twice daily, he might have to leave my classroom to take his medicine occasionally, which I need to be informed of throughout my time with Vinod.

Post-Secondary Transition Planning Needs:

A significant priority in Vinod's IEP is preparing him and planning his post-secondary transition. I need to understand where Vinod is heading to help prepare him for his future. I need to communicate with Vinod's parents, Vinod and also the IEP team to understand what the goals are for his transition.

Community-Based Instruction – This involves teaching students skills in the community environments in which the skills will be used. Vinod has expressed interest in living away from home and working in the community. Community-based instruction would greatly benefit Vinod for his future. Typically schools are very involved with the community they are located in, and getting Vinod involved in those activities would be very helpful to him.

Extended School Year – This is not necessarily a strategy for the everyday classroom but a program run during the summer for students with disabilities to help them stay on track. During the summer months, some students have been known to regress and forget the information or knowledge they learned the previous school year. This program is a great way to support these students and help them keep progressing forward. This would help Vinod stay on track and keep up with his academics. This would also help Vinod stay socially active. For example, my school district has an Extended School Year, and some non-disabled students can volunteer their time during this program to run activities or play games with these students. It is an excellent experience for everyone involved.

Case Study of Emotionally Disturbed #6

Phani is a 10-year-old boy who enjoys football, swimming, and baking. He does not like art activities or large crowds. Phani has a good sense of humour, but he can be irritable. He fears new people and may become quiet and more reserved. His parents and teachers talk him through exposure to new people. Phani is highly verbal and speaks in sentences. Phani is above grade level in reading. He enjoys reading, and his favourite book is A Very Hungry Caterpillar. According to Phani, he dislikes writing. Most of his writing is simple sentences with many grammatical errors and trim detail. He also struggles with math, in which he is approximately 2nd-grade levels below. He has recently learned how to pitch left-handed. Phani has a medical diagnosis of childhood-onset bipolar disorder and an educational classification of severe emotional and behavioural illness.

He takes medication for bipolar disorder daily. He is currently on a new drug. Phani has a new baby Sister who is 11 months old. Phani has been increasingly disruptive over the past few months. He has verbal outbursts and pushes classroom materials onto the floor after being given an academic task during quiet work time. His verbal outbursts include yelling that he is not doing the assignment, telling a student to shut up, using profanity, and calling students names. His teachers feel they spend about an hour daily dealing with the behaviour. They usually respond to Phani's behaviour by scolding or initiating an office referral. School Classroom Environment Phani attends a regular public school. Phani is new to the school. Phani is in the 5th grade. There are 19 students in his homeroom classroom. Phani has 60 minutes in a resource SPED class with five other students. Phani also has one co-teaching segment for math. His teacher is very organized and structured. She is loving and understanding concerning Phani's needs.

Case study of Speech and language impairment. #7

Prakash has a "language disorder." This means that his language is developing unusually. He is not just doing what we would expect but just a bit later. Prakash also has "a speech sound or pronunciation disorder". This means that his pronunciation is complicated to understand. It is not developing in the usual way. Prakash might have "verbal dyspraxia". This means he might have difficulty coordinating his muscles to make speech sounds. We are still checking if he does have this condition.

Assessing Prakash:

The therapist has seen Prakash in his local health centre, at home and nursery. She checked his play and attention skills and learned about his general development. She studied his understanding. She also assessed his pronunciation (speech sounds).

What we talked about with his parents

The therapist found out that Prakash understood what people said very well. He had difficulty putting words together in sentences. He had trouble saying words clearly so that other people could understand him. The therapist talked to his parents and said that

Prakash would need help from our service. She said he would need a long-term episode of care. She said Prakash would need help with his speech sounds and putting words together into sentences. She felt that he might need a communication aid to let other people know what he was trying to say. She also said Prakash might need help from other professionals and help in school. This might mean he needed to attend a school with extra support for children with speech and language difficulties.

What help Prakash gets:

Prakash gets lots of different types of support from his therapist.

- His parents and his school have attended a training run by our service to help them know more about speech sound difficulties and language

- He is learning Makaton signing – and so are his family difficulties. This will help him tell people what he is trying to say more easily

- He is practising his speech pronunciation

- He is using an Ipad with a unique app that turns it into a communication aid

- He is going to see a paediatrician

- He is going to be assessed to see if he needs extra support in school (Statutory Assessment)

- All the people involved with Prakash are meeting together to talk about what help he needs (Common Assessment Framework – Team Around the Child Meeting)

What's happening at the moment:

The therapist sees James for an ongoing episode of care. This is because he has severe communication difficulties. He might be referred to the Hospital Centre for an assessment because they specialise in dyspraxia.

Case Study Of Hearing Impairment: #8

This is a story of a little boy Hardeep in the village of Nadori. He has been identified with disabilities like hearing problems and speech problems. The little boy's mother is a homemaker, and his father is a farmer. The little boy was the third child of her parents and was born on 30 Sep. 2002. He had a typical birth, just like any other child. But as time passed, his health problems forced him to grow up to be a particular child. At the age of 4 years, he had fewer, so his hearing capacity became less. Doctors titled his problem as moderate hearing loss. The range of sounds the person can hear is only 40 to 69 dB. He is presently studying at a private school in Nadori, Fathehabad.

CASE HISTORY:

Name: Hardeep

Date of Birth: 30-09-2002

Father's Name: Mr Rajender

Mother's Name: Mrs Sharda

Language: Hindi

Religion: Hindi

Locality: Rural

Type of family: Nuclear

The problem in a child: Hearing impairment, Speech impairment

Issue noticed: 4 years of age

Cause of disability: Fever

Birthplace: Home, M.P. Rohi

Delivery: normal birth with an average cry. Birth weight: normal

Immunization: immunization of both mother as well as baby

FINDINGS

He was excellent and healthy until the fever, and there were no issues during or after his birth. There was no infection or other damage present at birth. He needs assistance participating in class and finishing his classwork because he struggles with vocabulary and language skills. He needs to keep working on his problem-solving abilities because he finds it challenging to resolve conflicts. Hardeep frequently misunderstands what is said and struggles to comprehend the teacher's instructions. He might make mistakes in his classwork or get so frustrated that he can't start or work on a task. He isolates himself from those around him when angry and does nothing.

He was not able to hear. He had to react at all things, although he wanted to reach them. Later, advised by doctors to go for speech therapy, his parents came with the child for treatment. He was soon put up in the speech therapy department.

The most significant aspect was expressing himself linguistically in the most basic forms from a young age. Lack of this ability can cause psychological and personality issues. So parents began conversing with him and singing nursery rhymes with him, just like all parents do, but Hardeep's mother also added signs and finger spelling.

He could briefly describe fifteen things when he was 4.5 years old. His lexicon expanded. When he was five years old, his parents put him in preschool. Despite having an 85-decibel loss in both ears across the entire frequency range, his hearing aid worked wonders, and he responded to speech more and showed a willingness to learn words.

Once his vocabulary was improved, he was trained for short sentences. As he learnt an ordinary word, he even improved his speech. He was now able to hear from the front and speak some sentences. Now he can listen to using hearing aids and explain his points to his parents. Now, this completes his journey to reach from staring.

CONCLUSION

Hardeep is a little boy who has hearing and speech disabilities. A partial or complete inability to hear is hearing loss or hearing impairment. A person who is deaf has minimal to no hearing. Hearing loss can distress one or both ears. Hearing issues can hinder a child's ability to learn spoken language and make it difficult for adults to perform their job duties. Hearing loss can make some people feel lonely, especially older people. Hearing loss can be either temporary or permanent. The importance of ear care, early intervention, education, and equal opportunities for children with hearing loss must be emphasized. Parents and children's lives can be significantly improved by educating all health professionals, parents, and teachers and creating specialized services. It's critical to keep pushing back against the expectations that parents of hearing-impaired children have for their children.

1234
ABCDEFGH
JKLMNOP
VWXYZ

Case Study of other health Impairments: #9

Background:

Leena was diagnosed with cancer about a year ago, currently in 9th grade at school.

Access Issues:

Leena switched to part-time status after she became ill. Her medication had some side effects, including lapses in concentration. She wants to continue her studies. However, there are days when Leena is too tired or nauseous to attend classes. She also has a doctor's appointment every other week. Her course of study runs every quarter, and she quickly falls behind if she misses too many discussions. Leena also needs to watch her stress level, as that can cause some of her symptoms to worsen.

Solutions:

Before each quarter, Leena had informed her instructors of the situation and obtained a course outline and the required assignments before the classes began. She worked out a communication system with the instructors and her advisor to avoid getting penalized if she missed deadlines. If she cannot complete the coursework, she requests an incomplete grade and can make up the work within a specified period. Leena also has been using the notetaking service, which sends lecture notes online following each session. In addition, she has made arrangements with one of the librarians to manage document requests for her and to send them by postal mail when she cannot come to the library.

Conclusion:

This example illustrates:

1. The importance of instructor flexibility and a self-paced instructional option.

2. How can support accessing materials and information be provided when a student cannot be physically present?

3. The active role a student can play in coordinating her support services.

Case Study of Deafblindness: #10

Sendil is a 15-year-old high school student participating in the model demonstration project since 2003. Since the beginning, Sendil's mother and home care providers have played a critical role in helping him realize success. When the project began in 2003, Sendil had no formal means of communication, and his school program focused mainly on developing functional skills. Our efforts began with identifying a means of communication and a tool for writing.

We began exploring light-tech communication systems. Our first efforts involved a 4-location flip chart. In this video, you see Sendil using a combination of partner-assisted scanning and eye-pointing to make choices. This is the first time Sendil and his mom have tried this system.

Watching Sendil use the 4-location flip chart with eye-pointing helped us evaluate his vision and understanding of symbols. It became clear that he could visually distinguish between characters in the library.

While we continued to explore light-tech solutions, we started exploring switch access.

Sendil had years of trials with single switches without much success. Efforts with 2-switch step scanning proved much more successful for him. He uses his arm to move the highlighter from one item to the next and his knee to select desired options.

It was evident that 2-switch step scanning would provide Sendil with a vital way to interact with technology and control partner-assisted scanning interactions. Based on our understanding of Sendil's vision and his use of 2-switch scanning, we tried several computer-based options for accessing the alphabet and writing. Ultimately, a light-tech solution provided the best support for Sendil in his early writing efforts.

A light-tech flip chart was the best way for Sendil to access the alphabet. Using this alternative pencil, Sendil could indicate which letters his partner should write for him. Sendil used his arm to access the mover switch, which lit a green light indicating that his partner should move to the following letter. When his partner pointed to a desired letter, Sendil used his knee to access the picker switch, which lit a red light indicating that his partner should write that letter for him.

Throughout the year, Sendil engaged in self-selected writing using the alphabet flip chart at home. He selected the topics for his writing and wrote in a journal or wrote notes to family and friends. The flip chart displays the letters of the alphabet in groups of 4 or 6 and offers simple editing commands such as space, new words, and delete.

In the following writing samples, facilitators always began the writing activity by supporting Sendil in selecting a topic. Choices were presented to Sendil via photographs, signs, and his remnant book. The remnant book was frequently his favourite as it documented the events of his life, big and small. Remnant books are typically used to set a topic for communication and are developed by collecting items from the activities and events Sendil experiences each day. For example, Sendil's remnant book includes ticket stubs from a movie he saw with his brother, a plastic bag with a dead bug he found, a picture cut from a game's box, and so on. Sendil selected a topic from the book by directing the facilitator to "go to the next page" using the switch by his arm and stop on the desired topic using the control by his leg to say, "that's the one I want."

Working with Sendil to help him select a topic is integral to his writing process. Beyond making it clear that we write for a purpose, setting a case provides us with the necessary information that supports our efforts to interpret his writing efforts. Since Sendil cannot tell us what he has written, knowledge of the topic helps us carefully consider the letters Sendil selects and the words he attempts to spell. When we know the issue, we can attribute meaning to his writing attempts more successfully.

Sendil's early writing samples reflect his exploration of working with the whole alphabet and using the alternative pencil, the alphabet flip chart. In contrast, his initial attempts appear random, consistent and meaningful opportunities to write lead to change over time.

Over time, Sendil's writing began to show evidence of his increasing understanding of print. We see more evidence of first-letter knowledge. While we can't know with certainty that Sendil intended to write the words we believe he was writing, he eagerly confirms our inquiries occasionally and tells us no to others. For example, in this entry, Sendil wrote about a new friend named Ramesh. When asked, he confirmed that he was attempting to register his name, SE and Ramesh's name, R.

With time, Sendil continued to show evidence of more deliberate efforts to select particular letters in his writing. In this sample, he wrote about his mother, who was away for two weeks. This was a critical topic for Sendil as he has never been separated from his Mom for long periods. Again, he confirmed his attempts to write his name more than once "Send" and "Sddl" He also confirmed that he was writing about his mom, mmmmuuuu.

Within a few months of beginning to represent multiple words using initial letters, Sendil inserts spaces in his writing. He also begins to include words that are spelt correctly, dad.

Over time, Sendil's writing offers valuable, concrete evidence of his developing understanding of print. Writing is essential for students who cannot use gestures (pointing to individual words on the page), words (labelling letters and comments), and other behaviours to communicate their understanding of print. The alphabet flip chart provided Sendil with an alternative pencil that made writing every day a possibility.

Case Study of Orthopaedic Impairment: #11

Orthopaedic impairment is a severe impairment that adversely affects a child's educational performance. The term includes impairments caused by congenital anomaly (e.g., clubfoot, absence of some member, etc.), impairments caused by disease (e.g., poliomyelitis, bone tuberculosis, etc.), and impairments from other causes (e.g., cerebral palsy, amputations, and fractures or burns that cause contractures).

Characteristics

Orthopaedic impairments contain a wide variety of disorders. These can be divided into three main areas: neuromotor impairments, degenerative diseases, and musculoskeletal disorders. The specific characteristics of an individual with an orthopaedic impairment will depend on the particular illness, its severity, and additional individual factors.

A neuromotor impairment is an abnormality of, or damage to, the brain, spinal cord, or nervous system that sends impulses to the body's muscles. These impairments are acquired at or before birth, often resulting in complex motor problems affecting several body systems. These motor problems can include limited limb movement, loss of urinary control, and loss of proper spine alignment. The two most common neuromotor impairments are cerebral palsy and Spina Bifida.

Impact on Learning

The specific impact on an individual's learning depends on the disease's severity and individual factors. Two individuals with identical diagnoses may be quite different in terms of their capabilities.

Many students with orthopaedic impairments have no cognitive, learning, perceptual, language, or sensory issues. However, individuals with neuromotor impairments have a higher incidence of additional impairments, especially when there has been brain involvement. For most students with orthopaedic impairments, the impact on learning is focused on accommodations necessary for students to access academic instruction.

Imran, a little boy from Bangalore, had an Orthopedic impairment for which the following was implemented.

CASE STUDY ON *Developmental #12*

Our school operates under the premise that each student is unique and distinct. There can be no two precisely similar children. Some children are active, and then some youngsters are maybe hyperactive. Sameer Singh Bindra, who joined Kunwar's Global School family in 2019, is an example of a student who fits this description and attends our institution. When he first started school, he was a very demanding youngster who often lost his temper, had tantrums, and disrupted other children in various ways. After upsetting other people and acting poorly, he found it impossible to forgive himself.

We could get through to his heart if we handled the situation with a lot of patience. He is a young man who exudes an incredible amount of vitality. We tried to guide him in a more constructive direction with his energy and attempted to help him channel it. It was a tremendous motivating leap for him to realize himself and his talents when we applauded and acknowledged every one of his little efforts, and we did this consistently.

He is much calmer and more collected, and his social skills have improved significantly. He enjoys being generous with his possessions, particularly the meals he prepares. He is becoming more compassionate and kind at heart. He has the ambition of one day flying in space. In my opinion, he has brilliance. May the Lord continually bless him.

CASE STUDY ON Developmental #13

Every youngster has unique advantages. They may include aspects of their personality, their motor abilities, or the artwork that they create. Every youngster is uniquely capable in some way. We need to concentrate on what children are capable of doing, often known as their talents, as opposed to the limitations they may have. We can use children's skills to aid in the areas where they have the most significant difficulties.

Anantveer Awasthi, a student in the third grade, is a remarkable kid who has unique capabilities.

In 2020, Anant became a member of our family, and one of our priorities was to teach him reading and speech skills appropriate for elementary school. By the time we reached the middle of the session, we had all noticed that he was reading better and more attentive in class. The next thing that needed to be done was to assist him in improving his handwriting. With consistent encouragement and plenty of practice, he can now write as much as possible on as many different topics as possible. His self-assurance shone through as he performed on stage for the school's annual celebration. And as a result of all of this, he has even developed an interest in pursuits that call for him to use his creative side. He now has a passion for singing and dancing, and for Anant, reciting the Hanuman Chalisa is a significant achievement.

CASE STUDY ON Developmental #14

Whether hearing loss is mild or severe, there are plenty teachers can do to help students succeed. Ansh Pratap, a student in class 3, is exceptional as his eyes talk.
Ansh, with no formal training in Indian sign language, faced challenges in guiding him. So the first step taken was that the teachers voluntarily subscribed for sign language tutorials on youtube and simultaneously kept training Ansh too. A significant visible change was that he gradually understood little, if not all. Ansh started conversing without any hesitation with all his classmates, and other students, too, showed interest in learning sign language to make him feel more included in the class.

Conclusion:

Patience, small steps and continuous encouragement can make a huge difference in any student's life. Every child deserves a circle of inclusion and influence, but how we create is up to us all.

CASE STUDY ON *Developmental #15*

'Students don't care how much you know until they know how much you care.'
Sarv joined this school in the primary section. Initially, teachers were unaware of his problem. After learning about him, it was a challenge for the teachers of the primary team to teach him.

Earlier, he could not read and write like other students in his class. He roamed about in the class lost in his world, but with the teachers' constant efforts, encouragement and patience, Sarv has become keenly observant of his surroundings and things happening around him. He is in class six now. He still needs a solid push to write, but his rote memory has developed relatively well, and his command over Maths tables is appreciable.

Teaching Strategies

As with most students with disabilities, the classroom accommodations for students with orthopaedic impairments will vary dependent on the individual needs of the student. Since many students with orthopaedic impairments have no cognitive impairments, the general educator and special educator should collaborate to include the student in the broad curriculum as much as possible. For the student to access the general curriculum, the student may require these accommodations:

- Special seating arrangements to develop proper posture and movements

- Instruction focused on the development of gross and fine motor skills

- Securing suitable augmentative communication and other assistive devices

- Awareness of the medical conditions and their effect on the student.

Because of the multi-faceted nature of orthopaedic impairments, other specialists may be involved in developing and implementing an appropriate educational program for the student. These specialists can include:

- Physical Therapists who work on gross motor skills (focusing on the legs, back, neck and torso)

- Occupational Therapists who work on fine motor skills (focusing on the arms and hands as well as daily living activities such as dressing and bathing)

- Speech-Language Pathologists who work with the student on problems with speech and language

- Adapted Physical Education Teachers, who are specially trained PE teachers who work along with the OT and PT to develop an exercise program to help students with disabilities

- Other Therapists (Massage Therapists, Music Therapists, etc.)

Assistive Technology:

Due to the severity of orthopaedic impairment, multiple types of assistive technology may be used. As with any student with a disability, the assistive technology would need to address the student's need to access the educational curriculum. For students with orthopaedic impairments, these fall into three categories:

Devices to Access Information:

These assistive technology devices focus on aiding the student to access educational material.

These devices include:

- speech recognition software

- screen reading software

- augmentative and alternative communication devices

- academic software packages for students with disabilities

Devices for Positioning and Mobility:

These assistive technology devices focus on helping the student participate in educational activities. These devices include:

- canes

- walkers

- crutches

- wheelchairs

- specialized exercise equipment

- specialized chairs, desks, and tables for proper posture development. Constant monitoring does help in the long run.

THREE

TIPS TO PARENTS OF SPECIAL CHILDREN

The experience of parenting a kid with unique requirements may be fraught with difficulty but rich with rewards for the parents. Children with special needs may have distinct physiological, emotional, or developmental conditions for individualized care and attention.

The following are some helpful hints for parents of children with special needs, which will enable them to offer their kids the highest possible level of care and support:

Learn as much as you can about your child's condition. As the parent of a kid with a particular need, one of the essential things you can do is learn as much as you can about your child's condition. Find out how the disease is diagnosed and what treatment options are available. This might assist you in better comprehending the requirements of your kid and in advocating for their rights.

Get assistance: *While parenting a kid with special needs may, at times, be complicated and overwhelming, it is essential to seek help in this endeavour. Participating in a support group, connecting with other parents going through a similar experience, or visiting a therapist might fall under this category.*

Establish a routine: *Children with special needs can benefit from following a consistent daily schedule. They could have a better sense of being safe and in charge of their surroundings as a result of this. Create a daily routine that includes set times for meals, sleep, therapy sessions, and any other activities you want to* *participate in.*

Be patient: *Children with special needs may need more time and attention than typical youngsters. Be empathetic and patient with their specific requirements, and try not to be too harsh on yourself if things do not always go as planned.*

Honour their achievements: *While special children may have to overcome more obstacles than ordinary children, they also have great potential and have already achieved a great deal. Help children develop a healthy sense of self-confidence and self-esteem by praising their achievements, no matter how modest they may be.*

Promote the interests of your kid. *As the parent of a child with special needs, you are your child's most important champion. Raise your voice to support their requirements and rights, and collaborate with medical professionals, mental health professionals, and teachers to ensure they get the highest possible level of care.*

Accentuate their capabilities: *Rather than concentrating on your child's impairments, you should put more emphasis on their abilities. Assist them in identifying their qualifications and areas of interest, and make changes to pursue their ardent pursuits available.*

Take care of yourself *since the demands of raising a special needs kid may be taxing on both your body and your emotions. You must prioritize your health and well-being. Make sure you include time in your schedule for things that will help you take care of yourself, such as going to the gym, pursuing hobbies, or spending time with friends and family.*

Be adaptable: *children with special needs may exhibit unpredictability in their behaviour or call for modifications in the itinerary at the last minute. Have a flexible and adaptive mindset, and be ready to change your schedule as the situation warrants.*

Even though caring for a kid with special needs might be difficult at times, it is essential to make time to laugh and enjoy each other's company whenever possible. Create space in your schedule for fun and laughter, and value your precious time with your kid.

In conclusion, having a kid with a particular need may be an enriching experience, but, to do it successfully, one must have patience, devotion, and the desire to learn and develop. You can give the best possible care and support for your unique kid by educating yourself, finding help, establishing a routine, being patient, recognizing milestones, advocating for your child, stressing their skills, taking care of yourself, being flexible, and having fun.

About The Authors

Dheeraj Mehrotra, MS, MPhil, PhD (Education Management) honoris causa., a white and a yellow belt in SIX SIGMA, a Certified NLP Business Diploma holder, is an Educational Innovator, Author, with expertise in Six Sigma In Education, Academic Audits, Neuro-Linguistic Programming (NLP), Total Quality Management In Education, an Experiential Educator, a CBSE Resource towards School Assessment (SQAA), CCE, JIT, Five S, and KAIZEN. He has authored over 100 books on topics which include Computer Science, AI, Digital Body Language, NLP,

Quality Circles, School Management, Classroom Effectiveness and Safety and security in schools. A former Principal at De Indian Public School, New Delhi, (INDIA), NPS International School, Guwahati, and Education Officer at GEMS, Gurgaon, with an ample teaching experience of over Two Decades, he is a certified Trainer for Quality Circles/ TQM in Education and QCI Standards for School Accreditation/ School Audits and Management. He has also been honoured with the President of India's National Teacher Award in the year 2006 and the Best Science Teacher State Award (By the Ministry of Science and Technology, State of UP), Innovation in Education for his inception of Six Sigma In Education by Education Watch, New Delhi and Education World- Best Teacher Award, BOLT Learner Teacher Award by Air India, 'Innovation in Education Award 2016' by Higher Education Forum (HEF), Gujarat Chapter, among others. He has developed over 150 FREE EDUCATIONAL MOBILE Apps for the Google Play Store exclusively for Teachers, Students, and Parents. This work has been recognised by the LIMCA BOOK OF RECORDS & INDIA BOOK OF RECORDS as the only Indian to draw that feast. Dr Mehrotra is a PRINCIPAL at KUNWARS GLOBAL SCHOOL, Lucknow, India. He has conducted over 1000 workshops globally on "Excellence In Education" integrated with Total Quality Management and Six Sigma, Technology Integration in Education (TIE), Developing towards being ROCKSTAR TEACHERS, including Cyberspace, Cyber Security, Classroom Management, School Leadership & Management, and Innovative teaching within classrooms via Mind Maps, NLP and Experiential Learning in Academics. He is an active TEDx speaker and can be viewed on the youtube TEDx channel. As a premium

UDEMY Instructor, he has developed over 450 courses and caters to over 8 Lakh students from 180 countries. He can be visited at www.authordheerajmehrotra.com.

ÞÞÞ

Ms. Amita Pandit Bhatt has two decades of excellence in education, counselling and administration, she is a dedicated, resourceful and goal-driven professional educator with a solid commitment to every child's social and academic growth and development. An accommodating and versatile individual with the talent to develop inspiring hands-on lessons that capture a child's imagination and breed success. Ms. Amita is closer to her dream of educating the young minds of India. Since childhood, she has dreamed of dedicating herself to the field of education. She aims to render educated and able youth to the nation. A woman of integrity, rectitude, and a profound educator, the brain behind the case studies of students with disabilities. She believes in sustainable leadership and strives to build a professional learning community with all stakeholders. Amita's list of laudable achievements continues and amazes everybody around her. But one achievement she has is not just to be rewarded but also a giant leap for humanity. A village called Simrai near Abdullaganj, Rajdhani Bhopal, and 20 villages around it lacked girl-child education. The area had no schools and lacked any necessities of education. She and her team built a private school there and inspired and influenced the people around them to educate their girl children. After years of hard work and assiduity, the girls of those villages are doctors, engineers, and of many notable positions they wished for. Amita has the vigour to uplift students and fills them with enthusiasm for academic or non-academic education. Amita believes - *Her job is not to prepare students for something; her career is to help students prepare themselves for anything*. Amita aims to make studies and schooling simpler and better for children. Fighting the traditional norms, she is trying to bring methods that not only make the students brighter and remove constant educational pressure. Amita embraces the uniqueness of every single child. Amita believes that if every citizen dedicates a part of their everyday life to educating any underprivileged student, slowly but surely, they'll move towards fulfilling the dream of Aatmanirbhar Bharat.

Printed by Libri Plureos GmbH in Hamburg,
Germany